The Most Amazing Sports Stories of All Time for Kids

15 Inspirational Tales From

Sports History for Young Readers

Bradley Simon

Table of Contents

CHAPTER 1:

Air Majesty: Michael Jordan and the Chicago Bulls Dynasty

In the heart of North Carolina, during a time when the world was just discovering the magic of rock 'n' roll, a boy named Michael Jordan was born. Little did anyone know, this boy would grow up to redefine the world of basketball, soaring high above the courts, and capturing the hearts of millions.

Michael's early years were much like any other kid's. He lived in Wilmington with his family, played games with his siblings, and went to school. But what set Michael apart was an inner fire, a burning passion for everything he did. Whether it was a friendly game of cards or a competitive match of basketball, Michael played to win.

Basketball, however, wasn't his first love. As a young boy, he was passionate about baseball, influenced by his father, James Jordan. The two would spend hours playing catch in their backyard. It was a bond Michael cherished. But as time went on, the allure of the basketball court began to beckon him.

At Laney High School, a young Michael was eager to showcase his skills. But, in a twist that might seem like fiction, he was initially cut from the varsity basketball team during his sophomore year. They said he was too short. It was a blow, a harsh sting of disappointment. But instead of sulking, Michael used it as fuel. He practiced harder, pushed himself further, and grew not just in height but in skill and determination.

His dedication paid off. In his senior year, not only did Michael make the team, but he shone, quickly becoming a star player. It was clear to everyone watching; this young man was destined for greatness.

From high school courts, Michael went on to play at the University of North Carolina. It was here that he made one of the most iconic shots in college basketball history during the 1982 NCAA Championship against Georgetown. With just 17 seconds left on the clock and his team trailing, Michael took a shot. The ball swished through the net, earning the Tar Heels a national championship. It was moments like these that gave the world a glimpse of the legend in the making.

In 1984, a new chapter began. The Chicago Bulls, a team hungry for success, chose Michael in the NBA Draft. The Windy

City embraced him, and he embraced it right back. The arenas, which were once half-empty, began filling up. Fans flocked to see the new sensation, and Michael didn't disappoint.

The first few years were challenging. The NBA was filled with talented teams and legendary players. But Michael, with his unmatched work ethic and relentless drive, rose above them. He had an uncanny ability to hang in the air, defying gravity, earning him the nickname "Air Jordan." The moves he displayed were more than just sports; they were an art.

But as we know, basketball is a team game. And while Michael was a phenomenon, he needed a strong team behind him. Enter Scottie Pippen and later, Dennis Rodman. Together, they formed a trio that was almost unstoppable. With Coach Phil Jackson guiding them, the Chicago Bulls embarked on a journey of dominance.

Throughout the 90s, the Bulls were the team to beat. They won championship after championship, with Michael leading the charge. Off the court, Michael's fame skyrocketed. He wasn't just a basketball player; he was a global icon. Kids everywhere wanted to "Be Like Mike."

As the 1990s dawned, the Chicago Bulls were on the cusp of creating one of the most remarkable eras in sports history. With Michael Jordan at the helm, the team was not just winning games; they were making statements. Each victory, each play, each moment on the court was a testament to their skill, determination, and undeniable synergy.

Basketball aficionados knew the '90s Bulls were something special. The team's prowess was not just about Michael Jordan's brilliance, but a combination of factors that created an almost unbeatable force. Scottie Pippen, often referred to as Michael's right-hand man, was a force unto himself. His agility, his defensive capabilities, and his ability to read the game made him the perfect complement to Michael. They were the dynamic duo, and together, they navigated the rough and tumble world of 90s NBA basketball with finesse and flair.

Then there was Dennis Rodman. The man with the flamboyant hair colors and larger-than-life personality. Off the court, he was known for his antics and unpredictable behavior, but on the court, he was a rebounding machine. Rodman's ability to secure rebounds gave the Bulls numerous second-chance opportunities, a crucial factor in their championship runs.

Under the guidance of Coach Phil Jackson, the Bulls implemented the "Triangle Offense," a strategic play that emphasized spacing and player movement. This approach not only utilized Michael's scoring prowess but also harnessed the strengths of other team members, making the Bulls unpredictable and challenging to defend against.

The 90s saw the Bulls clinching six NBA championships, split into two 'three-peats' - a term popularized because of their back-to-back-to-back championship wins. Their first three-peat spanned from 1991 to 1993. These victories were more than just titles; they were a showcase of the Bulls' dominance.

However, after their third championship, a shockwave hit the basketball world: Michael Jordan announced his retirement from basketball in 1993. The news was staggering. The greatest basketball player was stepping away from the game. Michael's decision was deeply personal, stemming from the tragic loss of his father and a desire to try his hand at professional baseball, another sport he loved.

The Bulls, without their talismanic leader, faced challenges but managed to remain competitive. But the basketball world knew something was amiss. Then, in March 1995, a statement echoed around the world: "I'm back." Michael Jordan returned to the NBA.

His return brought an electrifying energy. The Bulls were back in full force. The team went on to secure another three-peat from 1996 to 1998. Their 72-10 record in the 1995-96 season remains one of the most impressive in NBA history.

Throughout these championship runs, the Bulls faced fierce rivals. The Detroit Pistons, known as the "Bad Boys" for their rough style of play, were one of the significant challenges in the early '90s. Then there were the Utah Jazz, led by the duo of Karl Malone and John Stockton, who faced off against the Bulls in two memorable NBA Finals.

The '90s Bulls became synonymous with excellence. Their games were spectacles, drawing in even those who weren't avid basketball fans. Everyone had a favorite moment: Michael's shrug after making six three-pointers in the first half against the

Portland Trail Blazers, his flu game where he played while being severely sick, or Steve Kerr's championship-clinching shot in 1997.

The curtain was beginning to close on the Bulls' magical run as the late '90s approached. The team, which had become an emblem of basketball dominance, was heading towards significant changes. But before that, there were still battles to be fought and championships to be won.

The 1997-98 season was particularly poignant. Rumblings suggested that this would be the last year Michael Jordan, Scottie Pippen, and Coach Phil Jackson would be together in Chicago. The season was aptly dubbed "The Last Dance," a term that later inspired the title of a famous documentary detailing the Bulls' journey.

Throughout the season, the pressure was palpable. Every game felt like an event. The Bulls, ever the fighters, rose to the occasion time and time again. Michael, even as he aged, showed why he was the best player in the game. His dedication, skill, and unmatched competitive spirit shone through, proving to the world that he still had the magic touch.

As the playoffs progressed, the anticipation grew. The Bulls faced off against a series of worthy opponents, each challenging them in unique ways. However, one matchup stood out: the NBA Finals against the Utah Jazz.

The Jazz, with their iconic duo of Karl Malone and John

Stockton, were looking for redemption after their loss to the Bulls the previous year. The games were intense, with each team pushing the other to the limit. It was a dance of strategy, skill, and sheer willpower.

Then came Game 6. With the series leaning 3-2 in favor of the Bulls, this game could seal their sixth championship. The final minutes of the game were heart-stopping. With the Bulls trailing by a point, the ball found its way to Michael. With his iconic poise, he made a move, pushing aside his defender and taking the shot. As the ball sailed through the air, time seemed to stand still. And then, swish! The Bulls took the lead and eventually won the game, clinching their sixth title in eight years.

The celebrations were euphoric. Yet, amid the joy, there was an air of finality. This incredible chapter of basketball history was coming to an end. Michael Jordan, after claiming his sixth Finals MVP, announced his retirement for the second time in January 1999. It marked the end of an era, not just for the Bulls but for the NBA.

While Michael would return to play two more seasons with the Washington Wizards, his time with the Bulls remains the most cherished. He left behind a legacy of excellence, dedication, and an unwavering commitment to the game. Michael Jordan wasn't just a basketball player; he was an icon, a global phenomenon that transcended the boundaries of the sport.

Young players around the world, whether shooting hoops in their backyards or practicing in professional arenas, looked up to Michael. They wanted to emulate his moves, adopt his work ethic, and capture even a fraction of his magic. He inspired a new generation, including many of today's NBA superstars, with his style, grace, and undying passion for the game.

The story of Michael Jordan and the 90s Chicago Bulls is more than just about basketball. It's about overcoming challenges, believing in oneself, and the power of teamwork. It's a testament to what can be achieved when talent meets hard work and determination. And for young fans everywhere, it serves as a shining example of how dreams, no matter how big, can come true with the right attitude and commitment.

CHAPTER 2:

Argentine Maestro: Lionel Messi's Dazzling Decade with Barcelona

In a small town called Rosario in Argentina, a little boy with big dreams kicked a soccer ball with passion and joy. Little did the world know that this boy, named Lionel Messi, would grow up to change the face of football forever.

Lionel's love for soccer started early. As a young child, he would often be found playing with his older brothers and cousins. Everyone who watched him could see he had a gift. The ball seemed to be a part of him, moving as though it was attached to his feet. However, life threw a challenge at young Lionel. At the tender age of 13, he was diagnosed with a growth hormone deficiency, which meant he wouldn't grow as tall as other boys his age.

But every cloud has a silver lining. FC Barcelona, a top football club from Spain, saw Messi's potential and offered to cover his medical expenses if he joined their youth academy, La Masia. Without hesitation, Lionel and his family moved to Spain, a big leap of faith that would pave the way for his legendary career.

Barcelona's La Masia is famous for nurturing young talents and teaching them not just about football, but also life values. Here, Lionel learned the importance of teamwork, discipline, and humility. It was also where he met some of his future teammates and friends, like Gerard Piqué and Cesc Fàbregas.

In no time, Messi's talent shone brightly, and it wasn't long before he was given a chance to play for Barcelona's main team. At just 17 years old, he made his official debut, and everyone could see that this young lad was something special.

As the years rolled on, Messi's influence on the team grew. Under the guidance of coaches like Pep Guardiola, he honed his skills, transforming from a promising youngster into a global superstar. But what was it that made Messi so special?

Firstly, his ability to control the ball was mesmerizing. It was as if the ball was glued to his feet! Whether he was weaving through multiple defenders or taking a shot at goal, Messi made it look easy. His low center of gravity, thanks to his shorter stature, allowed him to change directions swiftly, leaving defenders often bewildered.

Secondly, Messi's vision on the field was unparalleled. He could see passes and plays that others couldn't. It was this vision that led to many of Barcelona's goals, either with Messi providing the assist or finishing the play himself.

One of the most memorable periods for Messi and Barcelona was between 2008 and 2012. Under Coach Guardiola, Barcelona played a style of football that many consider the best ever. With Messi as the focal point, they employed a tactic called 'tiki-taka', characterized by short passing and movement. This was football artistry at its finest.

During this period, Barcelona won numerous titles, including the Champions League, which is Europe's top club competition. Messi, alongside teammates like Xavi Hernandez, Andrés Iniesta, and Sergio Busquets, displayed a level of football that left audiences worldwide in awe.

However, even in a team full of stars, Messi's brilliance stood out. He set records that seemed unbeatable, like scoring an astonishing 91 goals in a single calendar year in 2012. Each goal was celebrated with his signature move: pointing to the sky, a gesture in memory of his grandmother who introduced him to the beautiful game.

Barcelona fans were blessed to witness many iconic Messi moments. There was his magical solo goal against Getafe in 2007, where he dribbled past several defenders in a style reminiscent of another football legend, Diego Maradona. Or his unforgettable performance against Manchester United in the 2009 Champions League final, where he scored with a brilliant header.

While Lionel Messi dazzled on the field, it was his persona off the pitch that truly captured the hearts of many. Despite the blinding limelight that continuously followed him, Messi managed to maintain a low profile, making rare public appearances and often keeping his private life guarded.

Growing up in La Masia and transitioning to the senior team, Messi found more than just teammates in Barcelona; he found a family. The camaraderie shared with players like Xavi, Iniesta, and Gerard Piqué was evident both on and off the field. This bond strengthened the team's unity, playing a crucial role in their numerous victories.

Barcelona's Camp Nou, the iconic stadium, echoed with roars and chants every time Messi touched the ball. One could often hear the reverberating chants of "Messi, Messi!" as the entire stadium united in their adoration for their little magician. In return, Messi's commitment to the club was unwavering. Even during times of managerial changes, club politics, or unfavorable seasons, Messi's loyalty to Barcelona remained solid.

However, life at such great heights often comes with its set of challenges. In the world of sports, where every move is scrutinized and every performance is dissected, Messi faced his fair share of criticisms. Whether it was for a missed penalty or a quiet game, critics were quick to pounce. But, just like he would elegantly dribble past defenders on the field, Messi dealt with these criticisms gracefully, letting his game speak for itself.

His dedication towards improving and evolving was evident. He wasn't just content with being the best; he wanted to push boundaries. From being primarily a left-footed player, Messi worked on his right foot, making him unpredictable and even more challenging to defend against. He transformed from a winger to a false nine and later, a playmaker, showcasing his versatility and understanding of the game.

Amidst the trophies and records, Messi's relationship with the Barcelona fans was the real fairy tale. They watched a boy from Rosario grow into the world's best player right in front of their eyes. He celebrated joys with them, and they supported him during hardships. The connection was deeply emotional.

One of the most touching displays of this bond was Messi's tribute to the late Diego Maradona, an Argentine legend and Messi's childhood idol. After scoring a goal, Messi revealed an old Newell's Old Boys jersey, which Maradona had once worn, underneath his Barcelona shirt. This heartfelt gesture was a nod to their shared Argentine roots and the journey of two extraordinary players from the same country.

But like all good things, the Messi-Barcelona era had its challenges. Contract disputes, club management issues, and a desire for a new challenge led to whispers of Messi leaving

Barcelona. Fans around the world held their breath, hoping that their beloved player would continue his journey at Camp Nou.

Yet, deep down, many knew that whether Messi wore the Barcelona jersey or not, the memories, moments, and magic he created would forever be etched in the annals of football history. Messi wasn't just a player for Barcelona; he was an era, an emotion.

For children growing up watching Messi, the lessons were plentiful. Beyond the mesmerizing dribbles and jaw-dropping goals, Messi's story taught them about resilience, hard work, loyalty, and humility. In Lionel Messi, they didn't just see a footballer; they saw a beacon of inspiration, lighting the way for all who dared to dream big.

While Lionel Messi's saga with Barcelona painted a story of dedication, loyalty, and unmatched talent, his journey with the Argentine national team depicted a tale of perseverance, heartbreak, and ultimate triumph.

As with any great athlete, the weight of a nation's expectations lay heavy on Messi's shoulders. Argentina, a country with a rich footballing history, eagerly anticipated the moment when their prodigal son would lead them to glory on the international stage.

Early in his international career, the challenges were evident. Messi faced criticism from some Argentine fans who felt he showed more passion for his club than his country. They saw his incredible success at Barcelona and longed for the same magic to be replicated for Argentina. The pressure intensified with every international tournament, and the dream of lifting a World Cup or a Copa America trophy became the barometer of Messi's greatness in his homeland.

The 2014 FIFA World Cup in Brazil was a poignant chapter in Messi's international story. Argentina marched to the finals, with Messi being their beacon of hope, guiding them past formidable opponents. The stage was set in Rio de Janeiro against Germany. However, despite a valiant effort, Argentina fell short, with Germany clinching the title. The sight of a crestfallen Messi, receiving the Golden Ball award as the tournament's best player but without the World Cup trophy, tugged at the heartstrings of fans worldwide.

Subsequent editions of the Copa America brought more anguish. Finals in 2015 and 2016 against Chile ended in heartbreak. The weight of these losses bore heavily on Messi, who briefly retired from international football, a decision that sent shockwaves throughout the sport.

But true legends rise, and Messi is no exception. He returned to the national team, motivated by an undying love for his country and the dream of giving them the joy they so deeply craved.

Fast forward to 2021, the Copa America hosted by Brazil. Argentina, under the leadership of Messi, showcased a blend of passion and skill. Match by match, they progressed, and once again, Messi was at the forefront, orchestrating play, scoring goals, and inspiring his teammates. The finals saw a familiar foe, Brazil, but this time, the story had a different ending. Argentina triumphed, and Messi finally had his hands on a senior international trophy.

The scenes that followed were emotional. Messi, tears of joy streaming down his face, was swarmed by his teammates, celebrating a victory that was years in the making. The outpouring of love from fans, teammates, and even opponents spoke volumes about what this victory meant.

Messi's international journey offers invaluable life lessons. It's a story that teaches one to never give up, no matter the odds. To face failures head-on, learn from them, and continue pushing forward with hope and belief. Messi's tale with Argentina is a testament to the age-old saying, "It's not about how many times you fall, but how many times you get up."

As we conclude this chapter of Messi's career, we've ventured through his early days in Rosario, the majestic reign at Barcelona, and the roller-coaster ride with Argentina. Yet, Messi's impact is not limited to the football pitch. Off the field, he's a symbol of hope, a philanthropist, and an idol for countless children who lace up their boots, dreaming of emulating their hero.

CHAPTER 3:

Queen of the Court: Serena Williams' Dominance in Tennis

The sun glinted off the courts, and the crowd's murmurs gradually turned into a buzz of excitement. All eyes were fixed on one player, a figure of power, grace, and determination: Serena Williams. With each swing of her racket, she told a story of perseverance, resilience, and an unquenchable thirst for greatness.

Serena's tale began in the vibrant city of Compton, California. It might seem an unlikely place for a tennis legend to grow up. After all, Compton was known more for its hip-hop music and challenging neighborhoods than for tennis courts and serves. But for Serena and her sister Venus, this was where their love for tennis was born.

Guided by their father, Richard Williams, the Williams sisters began their journey on the uneven courts of Compton. They didn't have fancy equipment or world-class facilities, but they had a dream and an unwavering belief in each other. Their father saw the spark in them and believed that with dedication and hard work, they could conquer the world of tennis.

And oh, how right he was!

Serena, even as a young child, showed signs of the champion she would become. She was fierce, never backing down from a challenge. While many kids her age were busy with toys and games, Serena was out on the court, practicing her swings and serves, perfecting her game under the watchful eyes of her father.

But Serena's journey wasn't just about tennis. It was about breaking barriers. As a young African American girl in a sport that had few players of color at the top levels, she faced challenges that went beyond just her opponents on the court. There were whispers, doubters, and hurdles along the way. Yet, with each setback, Serena emerged stronger, using the challenges as fuel to push herself harder.

Her professional journey began at the tender age of 14. With powerful serves, agile movements, and a relentless fighting spirit, Serena quickly climbed the ranks. The tennis world took notice. Here was a player who brought a unique blend of power and finesse, shaking up the traditional norms of the game.

The early 2000s marked the beginning of Serena's dominance. Titles and accolades began to pour in. The Australian Open, Wimbledon, the US Open, and the French Open – the four Grand Slam tournaments, the most prestigious events in tennis – were all conquered by this force of nature. In fact, in 2002-2003, she held all four titles at once, a feat termed as the "Serena Slam".

Yet, what made Serena truly special was her ability to evolve. Tennis is a demanding sport, both physically and mentally. New players emerge, strategies change, and the game continuously evolves. But Serena, with her commitment to excellence, constantly adapted her game. She incorporated new techniques, improved her fitness levels, and showcased a mental toughness that left audiences in awe.

One of the most heartwarming aspects of Serena's journey was her relationship with her sister, Venus. Together, they took the tennis world by storm. Their matches against each other were epic battles, a blend of sibling rivalry and mutual respect. Off the court, they were each other's biggest supporters, always there to share a laugh, a hug, or words of encouragement.

However, like any true champion's journey, Serena's path had its share of bumps. Injuries, tough losses, and personal challenges tested her resolve. There were moments of doubt and pain, but Serena's spirit never wavered. She returned to the court each time with renewed vigor, showcasing her champion's heart.

Serena's influence wasn't restricted to the tennis court. She became a symbol of empowerment for girls and women worldwide. She showed that with hard work, belief, and passion, any barrier could be broken. Serena became a role model, not just as an athlete, but as a woman who stood up for what she believed in.

Serena's story is a treasure trove of lessons. It teaches about the importance of hard work, the value of believing in oneself, and the magic of perseverance. It shows that no dream is too big, no challenge insurmountable, as long as one has the heart to chase it.

Let's delve deeper into some of Serena's most memorable moments on the court, exploring the highs, the lows, and the moments that define her legacy.

One of the most iconic moments in tennis was unfolding at Wimbledon in 2008. There was a buzz of excitement that rippled through the crowds. On one side of the net was Serena Williams and on the other, her sister, Venus. The two shared a bond that went deeper than the sport. That day, the world watched as Venus triumphed, but it wasn't just a match; it was a celebration of their shared journey, of sisterhood and passion.

Flashback to the early 2000s, and Serena was already making headlines. In the span of a few years, she achieved something most athletes only dream of. Serena held titles from all four Grand Slam tournaments at once, not once, but twice. This 'Serena Slam,' first between 2002 and 2003 and later in

2014-2015, showcased her unrivaled prowess on the court. Holding the Australian Open, French Open, Wimbledon, and US Open titles in succession, Serena was nothing short of a tennis phenomenon.

Serena's Wimbledon victory in 2012 was a testament to her spirit. But what made it even more memorable was the joy that radiated from her. After securing the title, Serena couldn't contain her happiness. The tennis world watched, and many joined in, as she danced on the hallowed grass of Wimbledon.

However, every champion's journey has its valleys. In 2011, Serena faced one of her life's most formidable opponents, not on a tennis court, but in her health. A severe medical issue threatened her career, casting doubt on her return to professional tennis. But, echoing the lessons she'd taught her fans over the years, Serena showcased unparalleled resilience. Her triumphant return in 2012, crowned by her Wimbledon win, was more than a sporting victory. It was a win for determination, for heart, and for never giving up, no matter the odds.

Away from the spotlight of the tennis court, Serena had her superhero moment. One day, a would-be thief thought it wise to swipe her phone at a restaurant. But, much like on the court, Serena was fast and determined. In a flash, she chased the person and got her phone back. It was an incident that, in many ways, encapsulated Serena: quick-thinking, determined, and never one to back down from a challenge.

Life had another beautiful chapter in store for Serena. In

2017, she embraced one of the most profound roles of her life: motherhood. The world watched with adoration as little Alexis Olympia was introduced, often seen cheering for her superstar mom from the stands. For Serena, motherhood added another dimension to her life, making her story even more special.

Through every serve, every match, and every off-court moment, Serena Williams became more than just a tennis star. She became an emblem of hope, resilience, and sheer determination. Her story told of the importance of dreams, the value of hard work, and the beauty of perseverance. In her legacy, there's a message for every child: dream, work hard, and never let anything stop you.

In the history of sports, many names will shine, but Serena Williams' legacy will always stand tall, not just for her accolades but for the inspiration she instills in countless hearts worldwide.

CHAPTER 4:

Breaking Boundaries: Jackie Robinson Changes Baseball Forever

In a world where baseball diamonds sparkled under the sun and roars of fans filled stadiums, there was one player who changed the game forever. His name was Jackie Robinson.

Long before kids could look up to a myriad of sports stars from all backgrounds and colors, baseball, like many things in America, was divided. There were leagues for white players and separate leagues for Black players. The two never mixed. But Jackie Robinson was about to change all that.

Jackie was born in 1919 in Georgia, a southern state in America. Growing up, he and his family faced a lot of hardships. They were poor, and since they were Black, they faced prejudice and racism daily. But adversity often creates strength. Jackie's tough early years forged in him a resilience and a determination to stand up against injustice.

Jackie was a natural athlete. In school, he shone in various sports, not just baseball. He played football, basketball, track, and of course, baseball. His amazing skills earned him a spot on the University of California, Los Angeles (UCLA) sports teams, making him the first student ever to win varsity letters in four sports at UCLA!

However, despite his talent, Jackie lived in a time when the color of one's skin decided what one could and couldn't do. Even with all his achievements, doors of opportunity often remained closed for him. But Jackie was not the kind to back down.

During World War II, Jackie served in the US Army. He could have stayed away from the challenges he faced in America, but he chose to come back, to make a difference. After the war, he played baseball for the Kansas City Monarchs in the Negro Leagues. His undeniable talent and spirit caught the eye of Branch Rickey, the general manager of the Brooklyn Dodgers.

Now, Mr. Rickey had a dream. He believed that baseball, America's favorite pastime, should be for everyone, regardless of the color of their skin. He wanted to bring a Black player into the major leagues. But this was not just about baseball skills. Rickey knew that the first Black player in the major leagues would face scorn, anger, and perhaps even threats. He needed someone with extraordinary courage. And in Jackie Robinson, he found the perfect fit.

In 1947, history was made. Jackie Robinson became the first Black player to play in Major League Baseball when he stepped onto Ebbets Field for the Brooklyn Dodgers. The stadium buzzed with tension. There were cheers, but there were also jeers. Yet, every time Jackie stood at the plate or slid into a base, he wasn't just playing a game. He was challenging the status quo, breaking barriers, and paving the way for countless others.

The challenges were enormous. Jackie was often met with harsh words, aggressive plays from opponents, and even threats against him and his family. But Jackie had promised Mr. Rickey that he would remain strong and not react. And he held onto that promise with incredible grace and resilience. Instead of answering with words, Jackie responded with his talent. He played the game with such flair, skill, and passion that even those who were against him couldn't help but acknowledge his talent.

By the end of his first season, Jackie was not just another player. He was named the Rookie of the Year! And as years went by, Jackie continued to shine. He became the National League's Most Valuable Player in 1949 and led the Dodgers to win the World Series in 1955.

However, Jackie's impact went beyond scores and titles. He opened doors for Black athletes, not just in baseball but in all sports. Players like Willie Mays, Hank Aaron, and so many more followed in his footsteps, but they all owed a debt of gratitude to Jackie.

But Jackie wasn't just about baseball. Off the field, he was an activist. He spoke up for civil rights and worked to create opportunities for Black Americans in business and other fields. He was a beacon of hope, a symbol of what was possible when you believe in change and are willing to work for it.

In the pages of history, there are figures who shine brighter, whose impact resonates longer, and whose legacy inspires generations. Jackie Robinson is undoubtedly one of them. His story teaches us about courage, resilience, and the power of standing up for what is right. In a world where he could have been just a number, Jackie Robinson chose to be a trailblazer, forever changing the game of baseball and the world around it.

While Jackie's performance on the field made headlines, it was the strength of his character that made him a legend. Each time he put on his Brooklyn Dodgers uniform, he wasn't just playing for a win; he was playing for hope, equality, and a better future.

Children across America began to look up to him, seeing in Jackie a hero who stood tall amidst adversity. His baseball cards were treasured, and his games became events where families of all backgrounds would gather, sharing the excitement of watching number 42 in action.

Yet, for Jackie, the journey was about much more than personal accolades or game statistics. Every home run, stolen base, and strategic play was a statement, a message to the world about breaking barriers and the spirit of perseverance.

Behind the scenes, Jackie's life was a testament to resilience. At hotels, he was often denied rooms because of his color. During games, pitchers sometimes aimed balls directly at him. And the heckling from the stands could sometimes be harsh and filled with racial slurs. But Jackie bore all this with grace and determination. He once said, "I'm not concerned with your liking or disliking me... All I ask is that you respect me as a human being." And through his dignified conduct, he earned that respect, not just from fans, but also from many of his toughest critics.

Support also came in various forms. His teammates, who initially had mixed feelings about his inclusion, soon rallied around him. They witnessed his commitment, passion, and the injustices he faced. Many became vocal defenders, standing by him through thick and thin. The bond that Jackie shared with his wife, Rachel, was another pillar of strength. She was his rock, supporting and guiding him, reminding him of the larger purpose behind their shared sacrifices.

As the years rolled on, Jackie's influence began to reshape America's perception of sports and equality. Kids played baseball on streets and fields, dreaming of emulating their hero, Jackie Robinson. But his influence wasn't limited to baseball. He paved the way for integration across all sports. Athletes from diverse backgrounds began to shine in arenas of basketball, football, and more, all standing on the foundation that Jackie had laid.

After his retirement in 1956, Jackie remained an active voice in the fight for civil rights. He engaged with leaders like Martin Luther King Jr., championing the cause of racial equality. He also ventured into business and became the first Black television analyst in Major League Baseball. Jackie was breaking barriers, even off the field.

In 1972, the baseball world paid tribute to this incredible legend by retiring his jersey number, 42, across all teams. This was an honor never before bestowed on any player. Every year on April 15th, Major League Baseball celebrates Jackie Robinson Day, where players from every team don his number 42, a poignant reminder of his enduring legacy.

Jackie Robinson's story is a vivid tapestry of lessons. It's a tale that underscores the importance of tenacity, of standing up against injustice, and of believing in oneself even when the odds seem insurmountable. Jackie's life reminds us that while talent can make you a star, it's character that makes you a legend.

In the grand mosaic of sports history, many stars have shone brightly, but few have illuminated the path for others like Jackie Robinson did. Through his journey, he taught the world that sports isn't just about winning games, but about winning hearts, changing minds, and creating a world where dreams are limited only by the boundaries of imagination, not color or creed.

CHAPTER 5:

The Golf Prodigy: Tiger Woods' Historic Masters Win in 1997

In the sprawling greens of Augusta National Golf Club, where the chirping of birds often blends with the soft applause of spectators, a young man, just 21, was about to make history. This was the prestigious Masters Tournament, a place where legends of golf had walked, played, and left their mark. But 1997 was going to be different. It was the year of the Tiger.

Tiger Woods, with his trademark red shirt and unwavering focus, wasn't new to the world of golf. Born Eldrick Tont "Tiger" Woods in 1975, his journey with golf began when he was just a toddler. By the age of two, Tiger had already swung his first golf club, and by three, he had won a putting contest against the famous comedian Bob Hope. Yes, you read that right, at three years old!

His father, Earl Woods, recognized Tiger's prodigious talent and nurtured it. Earl, a former baseball player and Vietnam War veteran, introduced Tiger to golf. They would spend hours on the golf course, with Earl teaching and guiding his son, sharing both the techniques of the game and life's invaluable lessons.

As Tiger grew, so did his love for golf. During his teenage years, he broke and set numerous junior world golf records. The golfing world watched in awe as this young prodigy made waves with his extraordinary talent. Tiger's precision with the club, his ability to read the greens, and his competitive spirit set him apart. It was clear; a star was rising.

By the time Tiger entered Stanford University on a golf scholarship, his name was synonymous with excellence in the world of junior and amateur golf. But the professional arena was different. It was where legends were made. And in 1996, Tiger decided it was time. He turned professional.

Fast forward to 1997, and the stage was set for the Masters Tournament in Augusta, Georgia. The Masters is one of golf's most prestigious events, and winning it is every golfer's dream. The tournament's history was rich, and its traditions deep-rooted. From its iconic Green Jacket, awarded to the champion, to the beautiful yet challenging course, Augusta was a spectacle.

The air was thick with anticipation. Tiger, in his first Masters as a professional, was up against seasoned players, many of whom had been his childhood heroes. But if Tiger was nervous, he didn't show it. From the first day, he played with a passion and precision that left spectators and fellow golfers in awe.

Each swing of his club, each calculated putt, told a story of dedication and a dream. Tiger was not just playing to win; he was playing to inspire. And as the days progressed, it became clear that the young man was on his way to etching his name in history.

On the final day of the tournament, with thousands watching him live and millions more glued to their television sets, Tiger Woods achieved the incredible. He won the Masters, not just by a stroke or two, but by a record-breaking 12 strokes! It was the kind of victory that legends are made of. But what made it even more special was that Tiger was the youngest winner in the history of the Masters and the first person of African and Asian descent to win the tournament.

His victory wasn't just a personal achievement. It was a symbol of breaking barriers, of challenging the status quo. Golf, for a long time, had been viewed as a sport predominantly played and dominated by white players. Tiger's win changed that narrative. He showed that talent knows no color, and dreams are not bound by one's background.

As he wore the Green Jacket, awarded to him by the

previous year's champion, the significance of the moment was palpable. Here was Tiger Woods, a young man who had dared to dream, standing tall among legends, inspiring a new generation of golfers.

The impact of Tiger's 1997 Masters win resonated far beyond the greens of Augusta. Children across the world, many of whom had never held a golf club, were inspired. They saw in Tiger a hero, an icon, someone who showed that with hard work, dedication, and belief, anything is possible.

Over the years, Tiger Woods went on to win many more tournaments, facing ups and downs, challenges and triumphs. But the 1997 Masters win holds a special place. It was the moment a star truly shone, announcing his arrival in the world of golf and sports.

The story of Tiger's Masters win is more than just a sports tale. It's a lesson in determination, in believing in oneself, and in the power of dreams. It shows that no matter where you come from, no matter the challenges, with passion and perseverance, you can achieve greatness.

Tiger's legacy is one of unparalleled talent and unmatched determination. But most importantly, it's a legacy of hope, of breaking barriers, and of inspiring generations to dream big and chase those dreams with all their heart.

After the euphoria of the 1997 Masters win settled, the world began to see what a game-changer Tiger truly was, not just in golf but in the world of sports. His victory had already sent a clear message: barriers were meant to be broken, and ceilings were meant to be shattered.

With his charismatic smile, signature fist pumps, and undeniable skill, Tiger Woods quickly became a household name. Kids wanted to swing clubs just like him. Parents recognized in him a role model who exemplified hard work and dedication. Every golf course, driving range, and mini-golf park seemed to buzz with a renewed energy. And much of this excitement could be traced back to the young man with the iconic red shirt.

Tiger's influence extended off the golf course as well. He was not just an ambassador for the sport but also for change. He started the Tiger Woods Foundation in 1996, even before his historic win, with the primary aim of promoting golf among city kids and those who might not have the means to access the sport. But post his victory, the foundation's scope expanded. It began to provide educational resources, college-access opportunities, and STEM (science, technology, engineering, and mathematics) learning to underserved students.

While his win in 1997 had been historic, Tiger's journey had only just begun. Over the next few years, he clinched title after title, leaving an indelible mark on every tournament he played. His style, a blend of power and precision, challenged and often redefined traditional golfing wisdom.

Every major championship that followed saw Tiger as a

favorite. His approach to the game was meticulous. He didn't just play; he studied the courses, understanding every nuance, every twist and turn. This dedication combined with his natural talent made him a formidable force on the greens.

But what truly stood out was Tiger's mental strength. Golf, as any player will tell you, is as much a mental game as it is a physical one. And in this aspect, Tiger was unmatched. He could block out distractions, focus on the task at hand, and deliver under pressure. This mental toughness was evident in many nail-biting finishes and comeback victories.

One of the key aspects of Tiger's story is the influence of his family. His bond with his father, Earl, was special. Earl was more than just a father; he was a mentor, guide, and Tiger's most significant cheerleader. Many of Tiger's foundational lessons in golf and life came from him. They shared moments of joy, like the Masters win, and supported each other during challenges. When Earl passed away in 2006, it was a tough time for Tiger. But the lessons his father had instilled in him helped him navigate through this challenging period.

Tiger's impact on the world of golf is undeniable. Courses started being designed keeping him in mind, often termed "Tiger-proofing", to make them more challenging. Prize money in tournaments increased, thanks in part to the surge in viewership and interest Tiger brought to the sport. New generations of golfers, inspired by Woods, began to emerge, bringing with them a blend of athleticism and skill that has since become a staple of modern golf.

Throughout history, there are moments that define eras and players who become legends. Tiger Woods, with his 1997 Masters win, didn't just capture a title; he captured the imagination of millions. For every child swinging a club on a sunny afternoon, every student pushing through challenges, the story of Tiger Woods serves as a reminder of the magic of dreams, the value of hard work, and the endless possibilities that lie ahead for those who dare to reach for the stars.

CHAPTER 6:

Mamba Out: Kobe Bryant's Farewell Game

In the city of Los Angeles, where stars of both the silver screen and the basketball court shine brightly, a particular star had illuminated the city for two decades. His name was Kobe Bryant. The year 2016 was coming to be known for many things, but for basketball fans everywhere, it was the year they'd bid farewell to one of the sport's greatest legends.

Born in 1978 in Philadelphia, Pennsylvania, Kobe Bryant had basketball in his veins. His father, Joe Bryant, was a professional basketball player, and young Kobe would often accompany him to games, absorbing the magic of the sport from the sidelines. As he grew, so did his love for the game, and it was evident that he had a special talent.

Kobe's journey to basketball stardom began in earnest when he decided to skip college and jump directly into the professional league, the NBA, right after high school. It was a bold move, but then again, Kobe was always one to follow his heart. The Los Angeles Lakers, one of the NBA's most iconic teams, saw his potential and made him a part of their family.

Over the years, Kobe, with his number 24 jersey, became synonymous with the Lakers. He was known for his incredible work ethic, spending countless hours practicing, often being the first to arrive and the last to leave. His dedication to his craft earned him the nickname 'The Black Mamba'. Just like the snake, Kobe was fast, precise, and always ready to strike on the basketball court.

Now, let's fast-forward to April 13, 2016. The setting was the Staples Center in Los Angeles, a place that Kobe had called home for 20 years. This was no ordinary game. It was Kobe Bryant's last professional basketball game. After two decades of thrilling fans with his skills, dedication, and passion for the sport, Kobe was ready to hang up his sneakers.

But if anyone thought that this would just be a ceremonial game, a quiet goodbye, they were in for a surprise. The Black Mamba had one more show to deliver.

The atmosphere in the Staples Center was electric. Fans from all over had gathered to witness this historic moment.

Celebrities, fellow athletes, past teammates - the arena was filled with those who had come to pay their respects to the basketball maestro.

As the game started, it was evident that Kobe was in his element. With every basket he made, the crowd roared, and the energy was palpable. The opposing team, the Utah Jazz, were formidable opponents, but this was Kobe's night.

He drove to the basket, made impossible shots, and showcased the skill that had made him a legend. And then, something magical happened. Kobe Bryant, in his final professional game, scored a whopping 60 points! It was the highest score by any player that season. The Staples Center erupted in cheers. "Kobe! Kobe!" echoed throughout the arena.

The final moments of the game saw Kobe with the ball. As the clock ticked down, he made his last shot, and the buzzer sounded. The game was over, but the celebrations had just begun. Teammates lifted Kobe onto their shoulders, fans were on their feet, and there wasn't a dry eye in the house. Kobe had given them a farewell to remember.

After the game, in the midst of the celebrations, Kobe took the microphone. With his family by his side, he addressed the fans, thanking them for their unwavering support over the years. And then, in a move that has since become iconic, he ended his speech with the words, "Mamba out," dropping the microphone.

That night, a chapter in basketball history closed. Kobe

Bryant's farewell game wasn't just a testament to his skill but to his passion, dedication, and love for the sport and his fans.

However, Kobe's influence extended beyond the basketball court. He was a mentor to many young players, guiding them and sharing his wisdom. Off the court, he was a family man, devoted to his wife and children. He also ventured into the world of storytelling, even winning an Oscar for his animated short film, 'Dear Basketball', which was a love letter to the sport that had given him so much.

Kobe's tragic passing in 2020 left a void in the world of sports and in the hearts of millions. But his legacy lives on. His story teaches us the importance of dedication, hard work, and following one's passion.

Kobe's journey is a beacon of inspiration. It reminds us that with determination, commitment, and a love for what you do, you can achieve greatness. In the vast galaxy of sports legends, Kobe Bryant's star will forever shine the brightest, reminding us of the warrior who gave his all, till the very end.

In the aftermath of that unforgettable game, tributes poured in from all over the world. The basketball community, from rookies to legends, all shared their admiration and respect for Kobe. But it wasn't just basketball players; athletes from different sports, musicians, actors, and even world leaders took a moment to honor the legacy of the Black Mamba.

Stories about Kobe's mentorship began to surface. Younger

players spoke of times when Kobe would give them advice, sometimes even calling them in the middle of the night to discuss game strategies. It became clear that Kobe wasn't just passionate about his own game; he was invested in the future of basketball. He took players under his wing, teaching them not just techniques but also instilling in them a mindset of excellence.

Kids in playgrounds tried to mimic his moves, shouting "Kobe!" every time they attempted a shot. It wasn't just about emulating his skill on the court; it was about embodying the Mamba mentality - a mindset of relentless pursuit, of always striving to be the best version of oneself, in sports and in life.

One could always spot signs and jerseys in arenas, not just in Los Angeles but across the world, that bore Kobe's name and number. These symbols were a testament to his global impact. From China to Europe, from South America to Africa, Kobe's influence was universal. He had become an ambassador for basketball, bridging cultures and bringing people together through their shared love for the sport.

As years went by, the legend of Kobe's farewell game grew. People spoke of where they were when they watched it, how they felt seeing Kobe in his element one last time. Parents narrated the tale to their children, painting a picture of the electric atmosphere in the Staples Center that day.

But beyond the 60 points and the cheers, there was a deeper significance to the game. It encapsulated Kobe's journey. From a young boy with dreams of playing in the NBA to becoming one of the game's all-time greats, Kobe had always given his all. And in his last game, he left it all on the court.

Away from the bright lights of the arena, Kobe embarked on new journeys. He became an advocate for women's basketball, often seen cheering from the sidelines at WNBA games with his daughter, Gianna, who shared his love for the sport. Together, they dreamed of her one day playing in the WNBA. The bond they shared over basketball was heartwarming. In interviews, Kobe would often speak of Gianna's talent and passion, his eyes lighting up with pride.

Kobe also delved into creative ventures. His book, The Mamba Mentality: How I Play, gave readers an insight into his mindset and approach to the game. His storytelling prowess was further highlighted when he won an Academy Award for Dear Basketball, a poignant reflection of his relationship with the sport.

Reflecting on Kobe Bryant's legacy, it's evident that he was more than just a basketball player. He was a mentor, a storyteller, a father, and an inspiration. His drive, determination, and love for what he did resonate with people everywhere. He showed that success isn't just about talent; it's about hard work, perseverance, and a never-give-up attitude.

In classrooms, sports fields, and homes across the world, Kobe's story continues to inspire. It teaches us that challenges and setbacks are a part of the journey and that true greatness lies in rising every time we fall.

In the end, while scores and statistics might fade, legends live on. Kobe Bryant's spirit, his Mamba mentality, and his love for basketball will forever echo in the hearts of those who knew him, watched him, and were inspired by him. And so, while the warrior might have taken his last ride, his legacy is eternal, forever reminding us of the boy who dared to dream and the legend who made those dreams a reality.

CHAPTER 7:

Rumble in the Jungle: Muhammad Ali's Strategic Triumph Over George Foreman

In the vast continent of Africa, in the heart of the Democratic Republic of Congo (then known as Zaire), a story was about to unfold that would capture the imagination of people around the world. This wasn't just a boxing match; it was a spectacle, a clash of titans. The year was 1974, and the event was aptly named the "Rumble in the Jungle."

Before we dive into the electric atmosphere of that night, let's get to know the two main characters of our story: Muhammad Ali and George Foreman.

Muhammad Ali, born Cassius Marcellus Clay Jr., wasn't just a boxer; he was a phenomenon. Known for his lightning-fast moves, his poetic taunts, and his unwavering confidence, Ali was already a legend by the 1970s. He danced around the boxing ring, floating "like a butterfly" and stinging "like a bee," as he often said. But Ali was more than his boxing prowess. He was a symbol of hope, a voice against injustice, and an advocate for civil rights.

On the other side was George Foreman, a powerhouse of strength and skill. Foreman's punches were feared in the boxing world. Each blow seemed like it had the force of a sledgehammer, knocking out opponents with an ease that was both impressive and terrifying. By 1974, George Foreman was the reigning heavyweight champion of the world, having defeated some of the best in the business.

The stage was set for one of the most significant boxing matches in history. On one side was Ali, the former champion, looking to reclaim his title. On the other was Foreman, the unbeatable force, ready to defend his crown. The world watched with bated breath.

The city of Kinshasa was buzzing. Fans poured in from all corners of the globe. Celebrities, journalists, musicians — everyone wanted to witness history in the making. Local musicians played rhythms that echoed the heartbeat of the continent, and the air was thick with anticipation.

As the match began, spectators expected Ali to dance

around, to use his famous speed and agility against the might of Foreman. But to everyone's surprise, Ali did something entirely unexpected. He leaned back against the ropes, covering his face and body, and let Foreman punch him. Again and again, Foreman unleashed his fury, but Ali absorbed it all, shielding himself while occasionally throwing a punch or two.

This was Ali's secret strategy, one that would later be called the "Rope-a-Dope." Instead of trying to out-punch Foreman, Ali was wearing him out, letting Foreman exhaust his energy. Ali's taunts continued throughout, "Is that all you got, George?" he would ask, challenging Foreman's might.

Round after round, the pattern continued. Ali defended, Foreman attacked. To the untrained eye, it seemed like Ali was on the losing end. But as the rounds progressed, a change became evident. Foreman's punches started losing their power. He was getting tired.

By the eighth round, Ali's strategy became clear. He began to attack, targeting a now visibly tired Foreman. And then, in a moment that would go down in history, Ali landed a series of punches that knocked George Foreman out. The unbeatable had been beaten! Ali was once again the heavyweight champion of the world!

The crowd erupted in joy. "Ali, bomaye!" they chanted, which means "Ali, kill him!" in the local Lingala language. Ali had done the unthinkable. He had not only reclaimed his title but had also shown the world the power of strategy, patience, and self-belief.

The "Rumble in the Jungle" was more than just a boxing match. It was a testament to Ali's genius, both as a boxer and as a thinker. He had gone into the fight with a plan, and even when things seemed bleak, he stuck to it, showcasing the importance of strategy and resilience.

This historic bout is a lesson in perseverance and smart thinking. Ali teaches us that in the face of challenges, sometimes we need to think outside the box, to come up with innovative solutions. Strength isn't just about physical power; it's also about the strength of the mind, the ability to strategize and adapt.

The legacy of the "Rumble in the Jungle" continues to inspire generations. It's a story that goes beyond the realm of sports, resonating with anyone who has faced seemingly insurmountable challenges. It reminds us that with belief, strategy, and determination, even the toughest battles can be won.

In the grand tapestry of sports legends, Muhammad Ali's name shines brightly, not just as a champion in the ring but as a hero who taught the world to believe in themselves, to fight with both the mind and the heart, and to always, always float like a butterfly and sting like a bee.

As news of Ali's victory spread across the globe, reactions poured in. Muhammad Ali was not just celebrated as a boxing legend, but as an icon of hope and resilience. For many, his win was symbolic, echoing the broader struggles of the 1970s, especially in the realms of civil rights and personal freedom.

Young children everywhere replayed the fight in their backyards, trying to mimic Ali's strategy. They didn't just see punches and jabs; they saw intelligence, patience, and a game plan that went against conventional wisdom. Teachers, coaches, and mentors across the globe used the "Rumble in the Jungle" as a teaching moment. It became a lesson in the power of strategic thinking and the importance of believing in oneself, even when the odds seem stacked against you.

Back in the United States, Ali's victory was celebrated with parades and ceremonies. But for Ali, the win was personal. He had once again proven his critics wrong. Those who had doubted his chances against the formidable Foreman were left in awe of his strategic genius.

The fight also solidified Ali's place as a global icon. He wasn't just America's hero; he was the world's hero. His appeal transcended borders, languages, and cultures. From the bustling streets of New York to the remote villages of Africa, people celebrated the legend of Muhammad Ali.

After the fight, in his typical poetic style, Ali shared his feelings, "I told you I was the greatest. I've beaten the unbeatable. I've done the impossible." These words, filled with pride and conviction, became a rallying cry for everyone who had ever been told they couldn't achieve something.

Ali's relationship with George Foreman also evolved post the fight. While they were fierce competitors in the ring, outside of it, they shared mutual respect. Foreman often spoke about the lessons he learned from that fight, emphasizing the importance of humility and strategy. Over the years, the two champions would share many moments, reminiscing about their iconic bout and the impact it had on the world of sports.

However, the "Rumble in the Jungle" was more than just its immediate aftermath. It had long-standing implications for the sport of boxing. Promoters and managers began to see the value in hosting big fights in international locations, recognizing the global appeal of the sport. The fight also inspired a generation of young boxers, many of whom took up the sport hoping to emulate the greatness of Ali.

For Muhammad Ali, the fight was one of the many highlights in a storied career. He continued to box, taking on and defeating other greats, always with his signature flair and confidence. But beyond his prowess in the ring, Ali was also known for his activism and philanthropy. He used his fame as a platform to address issues of social justice, race, and religious freedom.

As the years went by, Ali's influence extended to realms outside of boxing. He became an ambassador for peace, traveling the world and meeting with leaders, activists, and common folks alike. His message was always one of love, unity, and understanding.

For young people, the story of Muhammad Ali is a multifaceted lesson. It's a tale of a young boy from Louisville, Kentucky, who dared to dream big, defying odds and naysayers. It's a story of a champion who used his platform to advocate for change and make a difference. And at the heart of it all, it's a testament to the human spirit's indomitable will.

As the sun set on Ali's career and he moved away from the limelight, his legacy remained intact. He left behind a world inspired and changed by his actions, both inside and outside the ring. And today, when children lace up their boxing gloves or step into a ring, the spirit of Muhammad Ali lives on, reminding them always to fight with honor, to think strategically, and above all, to believe in themselves.

CHAPTER 8:

100m in 9.58 Seconds: Usain Bolt's Lightning Strike in 2009

On the Caribbean island of Jamaica, where the melodies of reggae echo amidst lush green landscapes, a young boy named Usain Bolt was setting the foundation for a future that would dazzle the world.

Growing up in the tranquil town of Sherwood Content, Usain's early days weren't filled with dreams of global sports stardom. The laughter of children playing cricket in open fields and the soft whispers of the breeze through tropical trees were the soundtrack to his childhood. This was a world far removed from the intense spotlight of international athletics. However, amidst these ordinary settings, an extraordinary talent was taking root.

Usain's first brushes with running weren't on high-tech tracks but on these rustic roads and fields. Like many children, he loved playing, and what started as playful races with friends slowly evolved into something more significant. Word began to spread about the lightning-fast kid who could outrun anyone in Sherwood Content. But was local village fame the ceiling for Usain Bolt?

As school competitions began, it was evident that Usain was not just fast by local standards. Even when pitted against the best in schools across Jamaica, he stood out. His legs, which seemed too long for his age, gave him an edge, enabling him to cover ground with fewer strides than his competitors. But it wasn't just about physical advantage. There was a spark, a fire in his eyes, a drive that pushed him to always aim for the finish line, to always be the best.

Coaches took note, and soon, Usain was introduced to more structured training. At first, the transition was challenging. Moving from spontaneous village races to the discipline of professional athletics required adjustments. There were techniques to learn, regimes to follow, and, of course, the pressures of higher-level competition to handle.

However, what set Usain apart was his ability to blend his disciplined training with the sheer joy of running. He didn't see races as just competitive events; for him, they were celebrations of his passion. This unique perspective became his strength.

While others felt the weight of expectations, Usain danced — literally and figuratively. His pre-race antics, which included playful dance moves, became as iconic as his races. They showcased his spirit and the message that even in the most challenging moments, it's essential to find joy.

His journey wasn't without setbacks. Like any athlete, Usain had his share of losses, injuries, and moments of doubt. But with the support of his coaches, family, and the indomitable Jamaican spirit, he always bounced back, stronger and faster.

By the time the 2008 Beijing Olympics came around, Usain Bolt was no longer just Jamaica's sweetheart; he was a rising global star. His incredible performances there set the stage for what would be one of the most memorable moments in athletics history the following year.

The city of Berlin, steeped in history and culture, was about to play host to an event that would be etched in the annals of sports: The 2009 World Athletics Championships. Athletes from all corners of the globe descended upon the city, each bringing their own story, their own dreams. But among them, one story was eagerly anticipated – that of Usain Bolt. Would he be able to recreate his Olympic magic?

The atmosphere was electric. The 100m race, always a marquee event, was generating an unprecedented buzz. Fans filled the stadium, their eyes fixated on the track, waiting for the spectacle to unfold. As the sprinters took their marks, the air was thick with tension and excitement.

The gunshot announced the race's commencement. And in those moments, as the world watched, the story of Usain Bolt's legendary 9.58-second run began to unfold.

The seconds leading up to any 100m race are filled with a peculiar kind of silence. As the athletes settled into their starting blocks, each carried a world within them, a culmination of years of hard work, sacrifices, hopes, and dreams. But among these elite athletes, Usain Bolt's towering presence was undeniably magnetic.

From the moment the race began, it was clear this wasn't going to be just another sprint. Every stride Usain took was a masterclass in speed, technique, and sheer willpower. The audience, many of whom were on their feet, could almost feel the ground tremble as Bolt powered through.

As the racers neared the halfway point, a distinct change began to emerge. While everyone else seemed to be giving it their all, Bolt appeared to be in a realm of his own. His face, calm and focused, betrayed no sign of the immense effort he was putting into each stride. To onlookers, it seemed as though time had slowed down, with Bolt gracefully defying the very limits of human capability.

The final meters of the race were nothing short of magical. With every tick of the clock, anticipation grew. The world record was not just under threat – it was being shattered. Bolt charged through the finish line, arms outstretched, chest forward, with a time of 9.58 seconds gleaming on the digital display. A new world record!

The stadium erupted into a cacophony of cheers, applause, and pure astonishment. Cameras flashed, capturing the historic moment from every conceivable angle. Commentators worldwide scrambled for words, trying to describe what they had just witnessed.

But amidst the chaos, Bolt's reaction was the most heartwarming. He knelt on the track, taking a moment to himself, perhaps absorbing the magnitude of his achievement. Then, with the infectious joy he was known for, he began his celebratory dance, thrilling fans with his moves. The boy from Sherwood Content, with dreams as vast as the Jamaican sky, had made history yet again.

News of his incredible feat spread like wildfire. From TV screens in bustling New York cafes to radios in remote African villages, the name 'Usain Bolt' echoed, symbolizing hope, inspiration, and the boundless limits of human potential.

Back in Jamaica, celebrations were in full swing. Bolt wasn't just a national hero; he was a beacon of hope, proof that with enough passion and dedication, even the loftiest dreams could become reality. Schools declared holidays, parades were organized, and the iconic 9.58 seconds became a number every Jamaican child knew by heart.

For young fans around the world, Bolt's story was a source of inspiration. Here was a man who, despite facing numerous challenges, had risen to global prominence through sheer dedication, hard work, and a sprinkle of his unique charm. He had demonstrated that it was okay to be different, that enjoying the journey was just as important as the destination, and that with enough belief, the impossible could indeed become possible.

Yet, amidst the worldwide acclaim, awards, and accolades, Usain Bolt remained grounded. He never forgot his roots, often speaking fondly of his early days in Jamaica and attributing his success to the unwavering support of his family, coaches, and community.

The story of the "9.58" wasn't just about breaking a record; it was a testament to the human spirit's unyielding determination. It was a reminder that greatness isn't just about natural talent but is sculpted through years of effort, resilience, and an undying passion for one's craft.

The 2009 World Championships in Berlin sealed Usain Bolt's legacy not just as the fastest man alive but as a global icon whose story would inspire generations to come. And as chapters in sports history go, this one was truly golden.

CHAPTER 9:

Against All Odds: Simone Biles, the Gymnastic Prodigy of the 2010s

In the world of gymnastics, precision, agility, and grace meld together to create breathtaking performances. Athletes train for years, honing their skills to perfection for moments under the spotlight. But even in this competitive realm, every once in a while, someone emerges who redefines what's possible. In the 2010s, that someone was Simone Biles.

Our story begins in Columbus, Ohio, where a young Simone was born in 1997. The early years of her life weren't filled with the fairy-tale moments one might expect for a future star. Simone and her siblings faced challenges, as their mother struggled with substance abuse issues. As a result, they were placed in foster care. But destiny had a different plan for Simone. Her grandparents, Ron and Nellie Biles, stepped in, adopting Simone and her younger sister and providing them with a loving and stable home in Texas.

It was in Texas, amidst the warm embrace of her family, that Simone's gymnastics journey began, almost by chance. At the age of six, a daycare field trip took her to Bannon's Gymnastix. Mesmerized by what she saw, Simone started mimicking the older gymnasts, showcasing a natural talent that caught the coaches' eyes. Recognizing the potential in this energetic young girl, they sent a letter home suggesting she begin formal training.

Under the guidance of her coaches, Simone's raw talent began to take shape. She quickly progressed through the levels, with her powerful performances setting her apart. However, gymnastics, like any elite sport, demanded dedication and countless hours of practice. Simone, even at a young age, showed an unparalleled work ethic. Day after day, she trained, perfecting her moves, learning new routines, and pushing her body's limits.

But it wasn't just Simone's physical prowess that was remarkable; it was her spirit. Gymnastics can be an incredibly challenging sport mentally. The pressure to perform, the fear of injuries, and the intense competition can take a toll. Yet, Simone faced these challenges head-on. Her bubbly personality, infectious laughter, and unwavering positivity made her a favorite, not just among her coaches but also her peers.

As she entered her teenage years, it became evident that Simone was not just another talented gymnast; she was a prodigy. Her routines were filled with complex moves, many of which she seemed to execute with ease, as if she was defying gravity. It wasn't long before she began participating in national competitions, showcasing her skills on bigger stages.

At the age of 14, Simone faced her first significant test: the 2011 American Classic. This was her opportunity to make a mark, to show the gymnastics community that a new star was on the horizon.

The 2011 American Classic was a beehive of activity. Bright lights, cameras, buzzing audiences, and of course, incredibly talented gymnasts from all over the nation. For many participants, the competition was a familiar arena, but for young Simone, it was her first step into a larger world of elite gymnastics. While she was a powerhouse during practice sessions, competing on such a grand stage was a different ballgame.

Despite the mounting pressures, Simone carried with her an air of confidence. Her routines were practiced to perfection, and she knew her strengths. But more than that, she possessed an innate ability to focus, drowning out the distractions and zeroing in on her performance.

When her turn came, the audience watched with curiosity.

Here was a newcomer, younger than most and relatively unknown. But within moments of her performance, Simone had the audience spellbound. Her floor routine displayed not just her technical prowess, but also her artistry and flair. The way she moved, the height of her jumps, and the sheer joy she emanated left spectators in awe.

Simone finished the competition with impressive scores, marking her entry into the elite club of American gymnasts. While she didn't clinch the top spot, her performance was a declaration of her immense potential. Gymnastics enthusiasts and experts began to whisper her name, speculating on the heights this young prodigy might reach.

After the American Classic, Simone's training intensified. With a taste of elite competition, she was hungry for more. Each day at the gym became a mission: to be stronger, more precise, and ready for the challenges ahead.

2013 proved to be a pivotal year for Simone. She participated in the World Artistic Gymnastics Championships in Belgium, a significant global competition that would pit her against some of the best in the world. The event was a true test of her skills, resilience, and mental strength.

At the Worlds, Simone was nothing short of spectacular. She bagged gold in the all-around, floor exercise, and vault, making her a three-time world champion in her debut appearance! This was no small feat. The world took notice of the young dynamo from Texas, who seemed poised to revolutionize gymnastics.

But with greater recognition came increased expectations. Everyone was watching Simone now, waiting to see if she would live up to the hype or crumble under pressure. Simone, however, had other plans. She used the attention as motivation, channeling the energy to further refine her craft.

In her journey, Simone also faced setbacks. Injuries, occasional losses, and the tremendous pressures of being in the spotlight were challenging. There were times when the weight of expectations seemed almost unbearable. But through it all, Simone's resilience shone through. Supported by her family, coaches, and teammates, she faced each hurdle with determination, using every setback as a stepping stone.

As the 2016 Rio Olympics approached, anticipation was high. Would Simone Biles, the gymnastic sensation of the decade, be able to carry her winning streak to the most prestigious sporting event in the world?

The atmosphere in Rio was electric. Athletes from around the world congregated, representing their nations and hoping to leave an indelible mark on the annals of sports history. Within the U.S. camp, all eyes were on Simone. Her teammates, some of the best gymnasts America had to offer, looked up to her, drawing inspiration from her journey and her unfaltering spirit.

The gymnastics events at the Olympics were, as always, fiercely competitive. The world's best had gathered, each bringing years of training and dedication to the fore. But when Simone took the stage, there was a palpable shift in the atmosphere. Every leap, every twist, every landing was executed with a precision and flair that left spectators and fellow gymnasts in awe.

Simone's performances in Rio were nothing short of poetic. She seemed to float, defying gravity with her jumps, captivating hearts with her routines. By the end of the gymnastics events, Simone Biles had etched her name into Olympic history, winning four gold medals and a bronze. Her victories in the individual all-around, vault, and floor exercise showcased her versatility and dominance in the sport.

However, beyond the medals and the accolades, what stood out was Simone's character. In interviews, she often deflected praise to her coaches, her teammates, and her family. She spoke candidly about the pressures of competition and the importance of mental well-being, resonating with audiences worldwide.

Kids and aspiring gymnasts could draw countless lessons from Simone's journey. Her story was not just one of talent realized but of adversities overcome. She had faced challenges, both personal and professional, head-on, emerging stronger with each one. Her dedication, hard work, and unyielding spirit served as a testament to what one could achieve with passion and perseverance.

And so, as the Rio Olympics drew to a close, Simone Biles returned home, not just as an Olympic champion but as a beacon of inspiration. She had proven that with dedication, resilience, and a heart full of dreams, one could scale the loftiest of heights.

The tale of Simone Biles, the gymnastic prodigy of the 2010s, serves as a beautiful reminder: While talent can set you on the path, it's the heart, the hard work, and the spirit that define the journey.

CHAPTER 10:

The Patriot's Playmaker:
Tom Brady's NFL Legacy

In the vast world of American sports, few games capture the heart and spirit of the nation like football. Stadiums filled to the brim, roaring crowds, thrilling plays, and moments of sheer athletic brilliance define the National Football League (NFL). And within this realm of giants, a quarterback named Tom Brady carved out a legacy that will be remembered for generations to come.

Tom's story didn't begin with the flash and fanfare that many might expect of someone destined for greatness. Born in 1977 in San Mateo, California, young Tom was the fourth child in the Brady household. Growing up, he was passionate about sports, especially football and baseball. He'd spend hours in the backyard, throwing balls and dreaming of playing for his favorite teams. But little did he know, he was taking baby steps towards becoming one of the most celebrated athletes in American football history.

During his high school years at Junipero Serra, Tom transitioned from being a passionate fan to a dedicated player. Under the California sun, he honed his skills as a quarterback, learning the intricacies of the game. His dedication was evident, as he'd often be the first to arrive for practice and the last to leave.

Upon graduating from high school, Tom faced a significant decision. He was a talented baseball player and even got drafted by the Montreal Expos. But his heart was set on football. Trusting his instincts and passion, he decided to pursue football in college and joined the University of Michigan.

College years are transformative for most, and for Tom Brady, they were no different. Michigan had a competitive football program, and earning a spot as a starting quarterback wasn't easy. In fact, for the initial years, Tom spent more time on the bench than on the field. But instead of letting disappointments dishearten him, he used them as fuel. He trained harder, studied the game more intently, and continuously sought to improve.

By the time he reached his junior and senior years, his perseverance paid off. Tom became the starting quarterback for the Michigan Wolverines and led the team to several victories, showcasing his skill and leadership. His college years were a testament to the importance of patience, hard work, and self-belief.

However, the world hadn't yet seen the rise of Tom Brady. The real turning point came in the year 2000 during the NFL Draft. As rounds went by, Tom waited for his name to be called. It wasn't until the sixth round, as the 199th pick, that the New England Patriots chose him. Many overlooked him, considering other quarterbacks to be more promising or athletically gifted.

But the Patriots saw potential in this young player from Michigan. Little did they know, they had just acquired a gem that would shine brighter than any in the history of the NFL.

In his initial years with the Patriots, Tom played backup to the starting quarterback. But destiny had its plans. In 2001, due to an injury to the starting quarterback, Tom got his chance to lead the team. And boy, did he seize the opportunity! Under his leadership, the Patriots transformed. The team, which had previously faced challenges, was now playing with a renewed vigor and strategy.

With Tom at the helm, the New England Patriots began an ascent that would reshape NFL history. The 2001 season was a roller coaster of emotions, filled with close games, nail-biting finishes, and moments of sheer brilliance. Tom showcased not just his skills as a quarterback but also his leadership qualities, rallying his team, and infusing them with confidence.

And then came the crowning moment of the season: Super Bowl XXXVI. The Patriots were up against the St. Louis Rams, a formidable opponent. For many, the Patriots were the underdogs, but Tom and his team had other plans. In a game filled with suspense, the Patriots clinched victory with a field goal, marking their first Super Bowl win in the franchise's history. Tom Brady, the young quarterback once overlooked in the draft, was named Super Bowl MVP.

But this was just the beginning of the Brady era. As seasons passed, the Patriots, with Tom leading the charge, became synonymous with success. They clinched Super Bowl victories in 2003, 2004, 2014, 2016, and 2018. Each victory added to Tom's legacy, solidifying his status as one of the greatest quarterbacks the game had ever seen.

Yet, Tom's journey was not always smooth. Like all athletes, he faced challenges, both on and off the field. Injuries, team dynamics, and the ever-present pressures of being in the spotlight were hurdles he had to overcome. There were moments of doubt, games that were lost, and critics who questioned his abilities, especially as he grew older. But Tom's resilience was unparalleled. He viewed each setback as a lesson, coming back stronger and more determined.

Off the field, Tom became an inspiration for young fans and aspiring football players. Stories of his work ethic, discipline, and dedication to his craft were legendary. He wasn't just a player who relied on talent; he was a testament to the importance of hard work, continuous learning, and unwavering commitment.

Young readers could glean countless lessons from Tom's story. His journey taught that success wasn't just about moments of glory on the field; it was built on hours of unseen hard work, countless sacrifices, and an undying passion for one's dream. Tom's NFL journey, from being the 199th draft pick to becoming a football legend, underscored the age-old adage: "It's not about where you start but where you finish."

As years rolled on, Tom Brady became more than just a football player; he was an institution. Players came and went, records were set and broken, but Tom's legacy remained steadfast. His relationship with the New England Patriots, which spanned two decades, was a testament to loyalty, teamwork, and mutual respect.

Towards the later stages of his career, Tom made a surprising move, joining the Tampa Bay Buccaneers. Many speculated on how he would fare outside the Patriots' ecosystem. But, ever the maestro, Tom led the Buccaneers to victory in Super Bowl LV, adding another feather to his already illustrious cap.

As the chapter of Tom Brady in the NFL unfolded, it was clear that his was a story for the ages. A tale of dreams, determination, and the drive to be the best. His legacy wasn't just in the trophies he won or the records he set; it was in the indomitable spirit he embodied, inspiring countless young hearts to believe in their dreams, no matter the odds.

Tom Brady's journey in the NFL serves as a beacon of hope and a shining example of what can be achieved with passion, dedication, and a never-give-up attitude. And as stories in football go, this one was, without a doubt, legendary.

CHAPTER 11:

From Athens to the NBA Finals: Giannis Antetokounmpo's Meteoric Rise

In the bustling city of Athens, Greece, where old buildings tell stories of heroes from long, long ago, a new kind of hero was growing up. In a neighborhood called Sepolia, which wasn't fancy or famous, young Giannis was often seen playing basketball with a big smile on his face.

Giannis and his family came from Nigeria, and life in Athens wasn't always easy. Money was tight, and sometimes people looked at them differently because they were from another country. But none of that stopped Giannis. Whenever he had a free moment, he was out playing basketball. Even if his shoes were old and torn, he played his heart out.

Imagine a really tall kid, who could run super fast, jump super high, and had arms so long they seemed to stretch forever. That was Giannis. He wasn't just playing; he was soaring, laughing, and making everyone watch in awe. And the coolest thing? His neighborhood friends and family always cheered him on. They believed in him, and that made him believe in himself even more.

Soon, people outside his little neighborhood started to notice. They'd whisper, "Have you seen that tall kid play? He's magic on the court!" Giannis began playing in bigger places than just his local street, and his amazing skills were clear to everyone who watched.

Giannis wasn't just an ordinary boy; he had a dream. His dream was big, as big as the sky. He wanted to play basketball with the best players in the whole world. And to do that, he needed to go to a place where the stars of basketball shined the brightest: the NBA, in America!

However, dreams don't come true just by wishing. They need hard work, belief, and sometimes, a sprinkle of luck. Giannis knew this better than anyone. Every morning, as the sun peeked over Athens, he would already be practicing. Dribble, shoot, jump, repeat. And while he practiced, he imagined playing against his heroes in massive arenas filled with cheering fans.

Word started to spread far and wide about this wonder-kid from Athens. Basketball scouts, the people who search for new talent, began showing up to his games. They watched with wide eyes and dropped jaws. Giannis moved like lightning across the court, and his heart and passion were clear to see.

One day, a big opportunity came knocking. Teams from the NBA, where stars like LeBron James and Kobe Bryant played, wanted Giannis to join them. Can you imagine? From the streets of Sepolia to the biggest basketball stage in the world! But the journey was not going to be easy. America was far away, and everything would be new and different.

When he arrived in the U.S., he was drafted to a team called the Milwaukee Bucks. Now, while you might think of a cute deer when you hear 'Bucks,' in basketball, it's a team with fierce players, huge fans, and a rich history. And Giannis? He was the youngest player on the team.

Being the new kid is never easy. Imagine moving to a new school, where you didn't know anyone, and everything felt unfamiliar. Now, magnify that feeling a hundred times. That's how Giannis felt. The game was faster, the players were stronger, and, oh boy, the stadiums were enormous!

But Giannis had a secret weapon: his unbreakable spirit. Even though he missed his family, his home, and his favorite Greek foods (like gyros and baklava), he was determined. Each time he fell, he got up. Every time someone said he couldn't do something, he showed them he could.

He spent hours in the gym, practicing even harder. He

learned from his teammates, asked questions, and never gave up. And the magical thing? People started to love him. Not just for how he played, but for who he was. A kind, funny, hardworking guy who loved basketball and loved making others smile.

Games went by, seasons changed, and something fantastic began to happen. Giannis started to shine. He became the star player for the Bucks, winning games and breaking records. Fans wore jerseys with his name, and kids everywhere began dreaming of playing like him.

The boy from Sepolia, with dreams as big as the sky, was now an NBA superstar. And the most wonderful part? He still remembered where he came from. He'd often speak about his family, his love for Athens, and the lessons he learned playing basketball on its streets.

The NBA is not just any basketball league. It's a stage where legends are made, and heroes are born. For Giannis, every game was a new adventure. And like any hero's tale, there were dragons to slay—well, not real dragons, but challenges that seemed just as big!

One of the coolest things about Giannis was that no matter how famous he got, he remained the same fun-loving boy from Athens. He'd often share videos of himself trying American snacks for the first time or joking around with his teammates. It was clear to see that Giannis was more than just a player; he was the heart and soul of the Milwaukee Bucks.

Speaking of soul, did you know that Giannis has brothers who also love basketball? That's right! The Antetokounmpo family had basketball in their blood. His brothers, Thanasis and Kostas, often played alongside or against him, making some games feel like a fun family reunion!

As seasons passed, Giannis earned a nickname that made everyone's ears perk up: "The Greek Freak". But it wasn't because he was strange. Oh no! It was because his skills on the court were so incredible, so unbelievable, that they seemed almost...freaky!

Basketballs seemed to stick to his fingers as he made impossible shots. His long legs covered the court in just a few strides, and he could jump and touch the hoop without even trying! Fans everywhere, whether they were supporting the Bucks or not, couldn't help but cheer for him.

Soon, awards started piling up. 'Most Valuable Player' (or MVP for short) was one of the big ones. And guess what? Giannis didn't win it just once but multiple times! It was like getting the gold star on your homework, again and again. And while the awards were shiny and nice, Giannis always said that the real prize was seeing the smiles on the faces of his fans.

Kids all over the world started dreaming of being like him. Basketball courts, whether in big cities or tiny towns, echoed with shouts of "I'm Giannis!" as children tried to mimic his moves. And the best part? Giannis always had time for them. Whether signing autographs, sending shout-outs on TV, or even playing surprise games in local parks, he showed kids that dreams, no matter how big, could come true.

But dreams aren't just about winning games or getting awards. For Giannis, it was also about giving back. He remembered the times when he didn't have much, so he made sure to help others. He donated money, supported charities, and always said that the biggest win was making the world a better place.

In the whirlwind of slam dunks, roaring crowds, and flashing lights, one thing remained unchanged: Giannis' heart. The heart of a boy from Athens, who loved his family, cherished his friends, and believed that with hard work, any dream could soar.

And so, as our exploration of Giannis Antetokounmpo draws to a close, remember this: every hero has a story, and every story starts with a dream. And who knows? Maybe one day, kids will be shouting out your name, dreaming of being just like you.

CHAPTER 12:

Pinstripe Pride: Derek Jeter's Iconic Journey with the New York Yankees

In the heart of New York City, where skyscrapers touch the sky and dreams feel almost tangible, baseball has always held a special place. The New York Yankees, one of the most celebrated teams in baseball history, has seen many legends grace its field. But among those stars, one name shines particularly bright: Derek Jeter.

Born on June 26, 1974, in Pequannock, New Jersey, Derek Sanderson Jeter always had baseball in his blood. As a child, summer visits to his grandparents meant trips to Yankee Stadium. Little Derek would sit in the stands, eyes wide, watching his heroes play, not knowing that one day, he would be the hero for countless other kids.

During his high school years in Kalamazoo, Michigan, Derek was a baseball sensation. He wasn't just good; he was extraordinary. The way he fielded the ball, the swift, elegant swing of his bat, and his natural leadership on the field made it clear: Derek Jeter was destined for greatness. It wasn't long before the big leagues noticed this young prodigy. In 1992, a dream came true for Derek when he was drafted by the New York Yankees, the very team he'd idolized as a child.

Derek spent a few years in the minor leagues, honing his skills and learning the intricacies of professional baseball. With each game, his confidence grew, his skills sharpened, and the buzz about this young talent became impossible to ignore. The Yankees' leadership saw potential in Derek, not just as a player, but as the future face of the franchise.

In 1996, Derek Jeter officially donned the Yankees' pinstriped uniform, taking his position as shortstop—a role he would redefine over the next two decades. His rookie season was nothing short of magical. Derek showcased maturity beyond his years, handling the pressures of playing in New York with grace. That very year, the Yankees won the World Series, a testament to the incredible impact of their rookie sensation.

But Derek's journey was about more than just baseball statistics and championship rings. It was the way he played the game that captured the hearts of fans. Derek respected baseball. He played with a passion, a commitment, and a love for the game that was evident every time he stepped onto the field. He was the first to arrive at practice and the last to leave, always pushing himself to be better, always playing for the team.

Young fans watched in awe as Derek made impossible plays look easy. They tried to mimic his signature jump-throw from shortstop, marveled at his clutch hits, and admired the way he always tipped his cap to the crowd. Derek wasn't just a player; he was a role model. Kids across the country wore number 2 jerseys, dreaming of playing like Jeter.

Off the field, Derek was equally impressive. He handled the media with grace, always took time for his fans, and was involved in charitable activities, especially those focused on helping kids. He founded the Turn 2 Foundation, dedicated to helping young people avoid drug and alcohol addiction and rewarding those who excel academically.

As the years went by, Derek's legacy with the Yankees grew. He became 'The Captain' in 2003, a title that acknowledged his leadership on and off the field. Under his captaincy, the Yankees saw a new era of success, clinching several more World Series titles.

Yet, like all great stories, there were challenges and moments of doubt. Injuries, slumps, and the pressures of playing in the spotlight were constant companions. But every time Derek faced adversity, he responded with determination and grace, always putting the team before himself.

In the world of sports, few things are as challenging as maintaining excellence over a long period. But Derek Jeter wasn't just any athlete. With each passing season, he seemed to find new ways to surprise and delight fans. His dedication to the game and his teammates never wavered. Every game was a new opportunity to showcase his talent and determination, and he took advantage of each one.

One of the most unforgettable moments in Derek's career came in July 2011. The Yankees were facing the Tampa Bay Rays at the Yankee Stadium. Derek was just a couple of hits shy of a significant milestone: 3,000 career hits. The excitement in the stadium was palpable, with fans on the edge of their seats every time he stepped up to the plate. And then, in a moment that seemed scripted for a movie, Derek hit a home run, securing his place in the exclusive 3,000-hit club. The stadium erupted in joy, with fans and teammates alike celebrating the incredible achievement.

But what truly set Derek apart was his consistency. He wasn't just about the big moments; he was about every moment. He understood that baseball was a team sport, and while individual achievements were nice, the true goal was to win as a team. This ethos was perhaps most evident in his postseason performances. October, the month of playoff baseball, seemed to be when Derek shone brightest. His clutch hits, remarkable defensive plays, and leadership helped the Yankees clinch many a crucial game. Because of his exceptional performances in these high-pressure situations, many started calling him "Mr. November," drawing parallels with another Yankees legend, Reggie Jackson, who was known as "Mr. October."

But, like all journeys, even Derek's had to come to an end. In 2014, he announced that it would be his final season playing professional baseball. It was a bittersweet moment for baseball fans worldwide. The thought of the Yankees without Jeter seemed almost unimaginable.

His final game at Yankee Stadium was nothing short of poetic. It was a cool September evening, and the stadium was packed with fans wanting to catch one last glimpse of their hero in action. The game against the Baltimore Orioles was tightly contested, but as fate would have it, Derek found himself at the plate in the bottom of the ninth inning, with a chance to win the game for the Yankees. And, true to his style, he delivered a walk-off hit, sealing the victory for his team. The stadium was a sea of emotions, with tears, smiles, and endless cheers. Derek took a lap around the stadium, thanking the fans, his teammates, and the game of baseball for the incredible journey.

Though his playing days came to an end, Derek's legacy in baseball remains immortal. He finished his career with numerous accolades: 14 All-Star selections, five Gold Glove Awards, five Silver Slugger Awards, and, most importantly, five World Series championships.

To the kids who watched him play, Derek Jeter was more than just a baseball player. He was a symbol of hard work, dedication, and the belief that with enough determination, one can achieve anything. He showed that being a great player wasn't just about talent; it was about respect, humility, and always giving your best, no matter the circumstances.

Today, while the Yankee Stadium still echoes with the chants of "Derek Jeter," his story serves as a timeless lesson. It's a testament to what one can achieve with passion, dedication, and an unwavering belief in oneself. For the children of the future and those of today, the tale of Derek Jeter's iconic journey with the New York Yankees will forever be a source of inspiration.

CHAPTER 13:

Chasing Speed on Asphalt: Lewis Hamilton's Drive for F1 Glory

Racing cars might seem like child's play when you're using toy cars on a miniature track in your living room. But in the real world, it's a world of roaring engines, blinding speeds, and intense competition. This world is called Formula 1, and amongst its many legends, there's a name that stands out: Lewis Hamilton.

Lewis was born on January 7, 1985, in Stevenage, England. As a young boy, he loved cars— not just toy cars, but the real, loud, and fast ones. At a very young age, Lewis showed signs that he was not an ordinary child when it came to racing. His dad, Anthony Hamilton, noticed his passion and decided to support him. Little did he know, this decision would lead Lewis to become one of the most celebrated F1 racers of all time.

Lewis started with remote-controlled cars, and by the age of eight, he was racing go-karts. You see, go-karts are like mini race cars, but for kids. Lewis would zoom past others, making sharp turns and overtakes that left spectators in awe. It was clear that he was naturally gifted. With every race, he got better, honing his skills, and learning the art of racing.

But it wasn't all smooth roads for Lewis. Racing can be an expensive sport, and there were times when his family struggled to finance his dreams. However, with determination and a lot of sacrifices from his family, especially his dad, who worked multiple jobs, Lewis kept on racing.

As Lewis got older, his karting successes drew attention. At ten years old, in a suit too big for him, he confidently walked up to Ron Dennis, the boss of the McLaren F1 team, and told him that one day he'd race for his team. Dennis was taken aback by this young boy's confidence and wrote in his autograph book, "Phone me in nine years, and we'll sort something out."

But Lewis didn't have to wait nine years. His talent was undeniable. He climbed the ranks in the racing world, moving from karts to bigger, faster cars in different junior racing series, always proving his skill at every level. It was evident that Lewis was destined for the grand stages of Formula 1.

In 2007, a dream came true: Lewis joined the McLaren

Formula 1 team, the same team he'd approached as a ten-year-old. It was time for him to race among the best, in cars that went at mind-boggling speeds. The world was eager to see how this young driver would perform.

In his debut season, Lewis shocked the world. He didn't just compete; he challenged the best, finishing on the podium in his first nine races, a record for a rookie! The world had not seen such a talent in a long time. Lewis's precision on the track, his bravery in overtakes, and his sheer love for racing shone through.

But, as with any sport, there were ups and downs. While he displayed unmatched skill and grit, there were challenges, both on and off the track. Yet, with each passing season, Lewis rose, breaking records, and setting new ones. His battles with competitors were legendary, often coming down to nail-biting finishes.

Lewis Hamilton wasn't just making waves in the racing world; he was causing tsunamis. With each season, he collected wins, accumulating championships as if they were part of a growing collection. By 2020, he had matched the legendary Michael Schumacher's record of seven World Championships. For a kid from Stevenage, it was an unimaginable feat, and Lewis had made it a reality.

However, as much as he was celebrated for his prowess on the track, Lewis faced his fair share of challenges too. He moved to the Mercedes team in 2013, and while many questioned this decision, as McLaren was considered a more competitive team at the time, Lewis saw it as an opportunity. And true to his vision, Mercedes evolved into the dominant team of the next decade, with Lewis as its shining star.

The Formula 1 tracks of the world — from the glitz of Monaco to the night lights of Singapore — became Lewis's playground. He had a unique style of driving; it was both aggressive and smooth. He could overtake opponents in places where others wouldn't dare. And his ability to extract the maximum from his car, especially in challenging conditions like rain, was unmatched. There were races where he'd start from the back and make his way to the podium, displaying sheer will, skill, and determination.

But Lewis's impact wasn't limited to just racing. He began using his platform to champion various causes. Concerned about the environment, he adopted a plant-based diet and urged his millions of fans to be more conscious of their carbon footprint. He also became a vocal advocate for diversity in motorsports, pushing for more representation and inclusivity. When the Black Lives Matter movement gained momentum in 2020, Lewis was at the forefront, taking a knee before races and wearing shirts with messages calling for justice and equality.

His influence extended beyond the racetrack. Kids everywhere looked up to him, not just as a sports icon, but as a hero who stood up for what he believed in. In schools, youngsters would talk about Lewis's latest win, but also about the messages he shared, discussing the importance of equality, justice, and taking care of our planet.

As the years passed, Lewis's legacy became more than just his racing achievements. It was about breaking barriers, in a sport where few before him looked like him. It was about speaking up, even when it was easier to remain silent. And most importantly, it was about inspiring a whole new generation to chase their dreams, no matter the obstacles.

In the world of Formula 1, cars evolve, records are broken, and new stars emerge. But legends like Lewis Hamilton, they remain timeless. His story is one of passion, resilience, and a relentless drive to be the best. It's a reminder that with dedication and heart, any young dreamer can steer their destiny and, quite literally in Lewis's case, race towards their dreams.

Every time young fans watch a Formula 1 race, they'll remember the tale of a boy from Stevenage who loved cars. A boy who became a legend and changed the world of racing forever. And maybe, just maybe, they'll be inspired to chase their dreams with the same vigor and passion that Lewis Hamilton did.

CHAPTER 14:

Commanding the Court: Novak Djokovic's Tennis Dominance

I n the realm of tennis, where the play is as much about strategy and endurance as it is about skill, emerged a star named Novak Djokovic. Born in Belgrade, Serbia, in 1987, Novak's journey to tennis supremacy is one of determination, resilience, and an undying love for the game.

As a young boy, Novak was introduced to tennis by chance. At just six years old, while skiing in the Kopaonik mountains, he stumbled upon a tennis court and was instantly mesmerized by the sport. The court was run by Jelena Gencic, a Serbian tennis coach known for her keen eye for talent. Recognizing the potential in young Novak, she took him under her wing. Jelena noticed not just his natural ability with a racket but his dedication and determination. She once said, "This is the greatest talent I have seen since Monica Seles."

Growing up, Serbia wasn't the ideal place for a budding tennis player. The nation was riddled with political turmoil and economic hardships. Tennis facilities and equipment were hard to come by. But young Novak and his family were unfazed. They believed in his dream and did everything they could to support him. Novak often recalls practicing in an empty swimming pool during winters to keep improving his game.

As he blossomed into a teenage prodigy, it became evident that if Novak was to reach his potential, he would need to train abroad. With great sacrifice from his family, he moved to a tennis academy in Germany at the age of 12. There, he honed his skills, developed his unique playing style, and got a taste of what international competition felt like.

Novak's style of play is a blend of agility, power, and unmatched endurance. He can stretch like an elastic band to return balls, making him one of the best defenders in tennis. But don't be fooled – he's equally lethal when on the offense. His powerful groundstrokes, combined with his ability to read the game, often leave opponents scrambling.

It wasn't long before Novak made waves in the junior tennis circuits. As he started winning tournaments, the tennis world began taking note of this young Serb with a fierce competitive streak and a never-say-die attitude. His breakout year came in

2008 when he won his first Grand Slam title at the Australian Open, announcing his arrival amongst the tennis elites.

But the journey to the top was not without its challenges. Tennis giants like Roger Federer and Rafael Nadal dominated the scene, and breaking their duopoly was no easy task. There were moments of doubt, times when injuries plagued him, and periods where his form dipped. But through it all, Novak's resilience shone through. He believed in his game, trusted his training, and always found a way to come back stronger.

Novak's intense training regimen and his dedication to fitness played a pivotal role in his success. He could outlast opponents in long rallies and grueling five-set matches. His ability to maintain peak physical and mental shape, even in the most pressure-packed situations, set him apart. Off the court, he adopted a gluten-free diet and practiced meditation and mindfulness, all contributing to his game's mental aspect.

The tennis world was in awe as Novak started accumulating Grand Slam titles. The Australian Open, Wimbledon, the US Open, and the French Open – he conquered them all. By the 2010s, he had solidified his place as one of the "Big Three" in men's tennis, alongside Federer and Nadal. The trio's rivalries are stuff legends are made of. They pushed each other to the limit, producing some of the most memorable matches in tennis history.

While the matches against Federer and Nadal were always highlights, they were more than just games. Each one was a clash of styles, strategies, and wills. Federer, with his graceful play and sublime skill; Nadal, with his raw power and tenacity; and Djokovic, with his blend of defense and offense, agility, and determination. Their battles on the court were an amalgamation of art and athleticism, a testament to the sport's beauty.

One of the most iconic rivalries of the decade was between Djokovic and Nadal. Their matches were often intense and lengthy, with both players pushing themselves to their physical and mental limits. The 2012 Australian Open final was a perfect example. The two tennis titans battled for nearly six hours, making it the longest Grand Slam final in the Open Era. Djokovic emerged victorious, but the match was a testament to the sheer will and determination of both players.

But Novak's journey wasn't just about his rivalries. It was about breaking records, setting new standards, and continuously evolving his game. He became known for his ability to adapt, whether it was changing his serve technique or tweaking his playing strategy based on the opponent. This adaptability, combined with his unwavering focus, made him one of the most formidable players on any surface, be it the grass of Wimbledon, the clay of Roland Garros, or the hard courts of the US and Australian Opens.

Off the court, Djokovic's influence was equally significant. He was passionate about using his platform to make a difference. In 2007, he established the Novak Djokovic Foundation, aiming to support children from disadvantaged communities in Serbia, providing them with quality preschool education. Recognizing the role early education played in his life, he was committed to ensuring other children had similar opportunities. This dedication to giving back showed a side of Novak that was as admirable as his prowess on the tennis court.

But, as with any sports journey, Novak's career had its moments of trials and tribulations. There were times when injuries threatened to derail his progress. There were moments of self-doubt, especially when he faced a series of defeats. However, his commitment to the game, his relentless drive, and his belief in himself always helped him bounce back.

As children reading this, there's so much to learn from Novak Djokovic's story. It's not just about winning or being the best in the world. It's about the journey, the hard work, the sacrifices, and the continuous pursuit of improvement. It's about understanding that setbacks are a part of growth and that challenges can be stepping stones to success. Whether you're a budding tennis player, an aspiring athlete in another sport, or someone with dreams outside of sports, Djokovic's tale is a lesson in perseverance, dedication, and believing in oneself.

By the end of the 2010s, Djokovic had secured his place among tennis legends. With numerous Grand Slam titles under his belt and records that would stand for years to come, his legacy was firmly established. Yet, even with all the accolades and achievements, Novak remained grounded, always attributing his success to his family, his team, and his love for the game. A boy who once played in empty swimming pools in Serbia had, against all odds, risen to dominate the global tennis stage.

CHAPTER 15:

On Ice: Wayne Gretzky,

The Great One of Hockey

In the world of hockey, a sport renowned for its fast-paced action, chilling rinks, and the sound of skates gliding over ice, one name stands out above all others: Wayne Gretzky. Known as "The Great One", Wayne's story is as extraordinary as the records he set, and it all started in a tiny backyard rink in Brantford, Ontario.

Picture this: a young boy, not more than three years old, lacing up his skates for the first time. The cold of the ice could be felt even through the thick soles of his boots. With each hesitant step, Wayne began his lifelong romance with hockey, spurred on by dreams that were bigger than the makeshift ice rink his father, Walter Gretzky, built in their backyard. Walter, noticing his son's keen interest, decided to give Wayne a head start in the sport. Little did he know that he was nurturing a prodigy.

Growing up, Wayne's life revolved around hockey. But it wasn't just about playing the sport. It was the way he studied the game, watching older players, understanding their moves, anticipating where the puck would be next, and figuring out how to get it there faster. By the age of six, Wayne was playing with ten-year-olds, a testament to his exceptional talent and dedication.

His early years in minor league hockey were like a foreshadowing of his professional career. Wayne was not the biggest or the strongest player on the ice, but he was often the smartest. He had an uncanny ability to read the game, to anticipate plays before they happened, and to always be in the right place at the right time. It's said that hockey isn't just played with the hands and feet, but most importantly, with the mind, and Wayne was a mastermind on ice.

When he was only 10 years old, Wayne did something incredible. He scored an astonishing 378 goals in a single season of peewee hockey. Yes, you read that right—378 goals! News of this young sensation began to spread, and Wayne's games started drawing larger crowds. Everyone wanted to see the kid who skated like the wind and scored like lightning.

However, success at a young age didn't come without its

challenges. As Wayne's fame grew, so did the pressure. Opposing teams would often double or triple-team him, trying their best to shut him down. But Wayne was resilient. He quickly learned to use this attention to his advantage, setting up his teammates to score.

By the time he reached his late teens, the whole of Canada knew about Wayne Gretzky. Scouts from professional teams watched his games, and it was clear that the NHL was in his future. Yet, before he reached the big league, Wayne had a brief stint in the World Hockey Association (WHA), playing for the Indianapolis Racers and then the Edmonton Oilers.

The WHA was a smaller, rival league to the NHL, and it was here that Wayne began to hone his skills against professional players. It wasn't long before the NHL and WHA merged, bringing the Oilers, along with Wayne, into the NHL.

In the NHL, Wayne wasted no time making a name for himself. By the end of his first season, he had tied for the league lead in points, announcing to the world that a new superstar had arrived. But this was just the beginning of Wayne's illustrious NHL career. As the seasons progressed, Wayne not only broke records; he shattered them.

But it wasn't just the numbers that made Wayne special. It was how he played the game—with grace, intelligence, and a kind of magic that left fans and opponents alike in awe. He had a vision of the ice like no other, seeing plays unfold well before they happened. This skill, combined with his impeccable hand-eye coordination, made Wayne virtually unstoppable.

And while he was a force to be reckoned with on the ice, off the ice, Wayne was humble and approachable. He never forgot where he came from and always made time for his fans, especially the young ones who looked up to him.

In Edmonton, Wayne became the cornerstone of a dynasty. The Oilers, with Wayne leading the charge, won four Stanley Cup championships in just five years. But even with all the team success, Wayne continued to push himself, always looking to improve and setting new personal goals.

With every game, Wayne Gretzky was writing his legend, setting records that seemed insurmountable. From the most points in a season to the fastest to reach 50 goals, Wayne's name became synonymous with greatness. Yet, as with all tales of legends, there are twists and turns, and Wayne's journey would take him from the city where he became a star to new adventures in the vast world of hockey.

As the 1980s rolled on, Wayne's stature in the NHL continued to grow. While Edmonton and its fans adored him, his fame reached far beyond the borders of Alberta. He was not just an athlete; he was an icon. His jersey, number 99, became one of the most recognizable in sports. It wasn't just a number; it was a symbol of excellence, representing a player who had changed the face of hockey.

But with great success often comes tough decisions. In a

move that stunned the sports world, in 1988, Wayne Gretzky was traded from the Edmonton Oilers to the Los Angeles Kings. The trade wasn't just monumental in terms of hockey; it was a cultural shift. The best player in the game was moving from a Canadian hockey stronghold to Los Angeles, a city more known for its sunshine than its ice rinks. The news brought tears to many, including Wayne himself. Leaving the Oilers was like leaving family.

But, as always, Wayne took on this new challenge with grace and determination. He didn't just go to Los Angeles to play hockey; he went there to grow the sport. And grow it he did! Under Wayne's influence, interest in hockey exploded in southern California. Kids who had never seen an ice rink before were now lacing up skates and dreaming of becoming the next Great One. Arenas that used to be half-empty were now packed to the rafters with fans eager to see Wayne work his magic.

While in Los Angeles, Wayne continued to dazzle on the ice. He led the Kings to a Stanley Cup Final and broke perhaps the most significant record of his career: becoming the NHL's all-time leading scorer. The night he broke the record was electric. As he skated around the rink, holding the puck that had marked his historic goal, the crowd rose to its feet, not just in applause, but in sheer admiration. It was a moment that transcended sports.

Yet, the journey of The Great One was far from over. After his time in Los Angeles, Wayne had stints with the St. Louis

Blues and the New York Rangers. Each time he donned a new jersey, he brought with him the same passion and skill that had made him a legend. He never stopped giving his all, whether in practice or in the biggest games.

Throughout his career, Wayne faced challenges head-on, from adapting to new teams to evolving his game in a rapidly changing league. And while he experienced incredible highs, he also faced his share of lows. Injuries, tough losses, and the weight of expectation were constant companions. But through it all, Wayne's love for the game never wavered.

Off the ice, Wayne was equally impactful. He was an ambassador for the sport, always taking the time to sign autographs, mentor younger players, and promote hockey at every opportunity. He understood the importance of giving back, and his charitable efforts, especially with children, showcased his big heart.

By the time Wayne decided to hang up his skates in 1999, he had not only set numerous records but had changed the game forever. His retirement was an emotional affair, with tributes pouring in from all over the world. The NHL even took the unprecedented step of retiring his number, 99, league-wide, ensuring that no player would ever wear it again.

Wayne's story is more than just about hockey. It's a tale of passion, dedication, and the relentless pursuit of excellence. It's about a young boy from Brantford who dreamed big and, through hard work and determination, became The Great One.

And while his playing days are over, Wayne Gretzky's impact on the world of hockey—and sports in general—will be felt for generations to come. He truly was, and always will be, the heart and soul of the game he loved so dearly.

Made in the USA
Middletown, DE
01 December 2024

65791304R00060